STEPHENSON'
AND TH_
RAINHILL TRIALS

Richard Gibbon

SHIRE PUBLICATIONS

Published in Great Britain in 2010 by Shire Publications Ltd, Midland House, West Way, Botley, Oxford OX2 0PH, United Kingdom.

44-02 23rd Street, Suite 219, Long Island City, NY 11101, USA.

E-mail: shire@shirebooks.co.uk   www.shirebooks.co.uk

© 2010 NMSI Trading Ltd.

Every attempt has been made by the Publishers to secure the appropriate permissions for materials reproduced in this book. If there has been any oversight we will be happy to rectify the situation and a written submission should be made to the Publishers.

A CIP catalogue record for this book is available from the British Library.

Shire Library no. 605.   ISBN-13: 978 0 74780 803 9

Richard Gibbon has asserted his right under the Copyright, Designs and Patents Act, 1988, to be identified as the author of this book.

Designed by Tony Truscott Designs, Sussex, UK and typeset in Perpetua and Gill Sans.

Printed in China through Worldprint Ltd.

10 11 12 13 14   10 9 8 7 6 5 4 3 2 1

COVER IMAGE

An artist's impression of *Rocket* on one of its demonstration runs, pulling passengers in front of the assembled crowds at Rainhill. The similarity to a horse-racing meeting is easy to spot. Note that *Rocket* is shown with the infamous sloping firebox, which is in fact incorrect. (Mike Mumford and Mumford Books; commissioned artist Brian Molloy.)

TITLE PAGE IMAGE

The driving wheel of one of the Robert Stephenson & Co's replica *Rocket* locomotives. It shows the wheelwright's skill in accommodating the off-centre drive, and the spherical crankpin arrangement to allow for misalignment of the axle on rough track. (Adam Jefferson.)

CONTENTS PAGE IMAGE

Rocket's brass hand-engraved nameplate showing evidence of the rough and tumble of the locomotive's earlier life. This is one of the components that escaped modification and did appear in front of the crowds at Rainhill in 1829.

ACKNOWLEDGEMENTS

Thanks are due to Dave Burrows, Dave Moore, Derek Rayner, Don Whitfield, Dave Campey, Sarah Norville, Andrew Scott CBE, the staff of Search Engine at the National Railway Museum, Bill Parker and Geoff Phelps of the Flour Mill at Bream, Michael Bailey and John Glithero for permission to extract material from their two excellent publications about *Rocket*, and Deborah Bloxam and John Liffen at the Science Museum. Special thanks must go to Nick Wright of Shire Publications and, above all, to Angela Anning, my wife, for the encouragement and assistance they gave me in this, my first book. Without them, it would never have happened.

THE NATIONAL RAILWAY MUSEUM

The National Railway Museum (NRM), York is the largest railway museum in the world. Its permanent displays and collections illustrate over 300 years of British railway history, from the Industrial Revolution to the present day. The NRM archive also includes a fabulous collection of railway advertising posters charting the history of rail. Visit www.nrm.org.uk to find out more.

Shire Publications is supporting the Woodland Trust, the UK's leading woodland conservation charity, by funding the dedication of trees.

CONTENTS

INTRODUCTION

THERE IS no doubt that *Rocket* is a milestone in railway history. Its silhouette is familiar to people all over the world, including countless schoolchildren much too young to remember steam trains, let alone *Rocket* itself. But what was the special contribution of this strange-looking little locomotive to the extraordinary story of the railways of Britain and the world, and how has it become such an icon? The story of *Rocket* begins with a problem, and the need for a solution.

In the early nineteenth century Manchester was growing rich on the profits of its cotton industry, before becoming a city in 1838, but the town's inland position gave the mill owners a problem. Raw cotton was imported through the port of Liverpool, and the cost of transporting the 1,000 tons a day of raw material the 35 miles from Liverpool to the factories of Manchester was as much as it cost to get the cotton from America across the Atlantic Ocean. A railway for the transport of both freight and passengers, to supplement the poor turnpike roads and the Duke of Bridgewater's restrictive canal, seemed the obvious solution.

The Liverpool & Manchester Railway (L&MR) would transform the transport of materials and finished goods between the mills and the port, but it would also be the world's first passenger-carrying railway. However, it was not certain at the outset what would propel trains on this pioneer railway.

Today, we take for granted what railways can do, and how they can carry huge tonnages of freight and vast numbers of commuters. In 1829, though, railway steam locomotives were a non-proven and misunderstood technology. There were prejudices against steam travel on the grounds of the effect it might have on human beings, travelling at speeds never before experienced, as well as fears about possible effects on animals and crops in the surrounding fields.

The Stockton & Darlington Railway (S&DR) had operated successfully since 1825 as a public coal-carrying railway, but the lessons learned did not necessarily apply to the L&MR four years later. The S&DR was transporting

Opposite:
Terence Cuneo's painting showing the excitement that the opening of the Stockton & Darlington Railway is said to have engendered, two years before *Rocket* appeared.

5

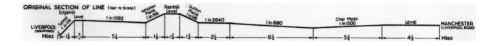

Above: The gradient profile of the proposed L&MR showing why the directors were keen to use stationary winding engines to raise and lower the trains on inclined sections.

Right: A map of the route showing how the bogland at Chat Moss, east of Rainhill, formed a huge obstacle to the building of the railway, which still follows the same course. The Manchester Ship Canal takes a route just to the south of the alignment shown.

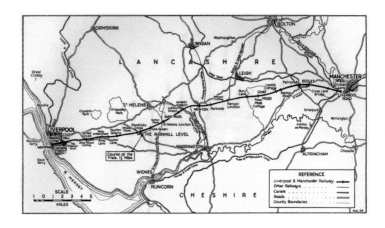

coal, mostly downhill, to the coast for shipment. Horses or locomotives would take the empty wagons back to the collieries. In contrast the L&MR was to be two-way traffic, carrying passengers and goods between two thriving centres of commerce. It was to become the world's first inter-city railway.

Choosing the right means of propulsion was of paramount importance to the directors, who intended their railway to be a moneyspinner for their shareholders. Inevitably the terrain was not flat and there were modest gradients that the trains would have to climb. Accepted thinking at the time

A train of colliery wagons negotiating the rope-worked incline at Seaham Harbour in County Durham some 160 years after George Stephenson argued that steam locomotives should replace rope-worked inclines for his railway. (Andrew Scott.)

was to have a series of stationary winding engines and ropes that would pull the ascending trains up, and lower the descending trains down the various gradients. While this may seem archaic and clumsy to us now, it was then regarded as eminently practical and, above all, proven. Indeed, it was a system that remained in use for many years: steam-hauled passenger trains were still being rope-hauled up the steep gradient out of Glasgow's Queen Street station as late as 1909, and freight trains were rope-hauled in the Peak District into the 1960s, and in County Durham into the 1980s.

George Stephenson – one of the pioneers of the steam locomotive – was the Chief Engineer of the L&MR and had surveyed the route of the new line. He believed passionately that steam locomotives could be used to operate the whole proposed railway, and in all likelihood tried to browbeat the L&MR directors into believing the same. In response, the directors took the unusual step of announcing a public competition to give the new steam locomotive concept a chance to prove itself once and for all. They offered a prize of £500 for the winner. They stipulated an arduous programme of duties for competitors to qualify, which became known as the 'Rainhill Trials' or, to the press, the 'Ordeal'. This programme, if completed successfully, would give the directors confidence that the steam locomotive was capable of powering their new railway without the use of fixed winding engines. Thus the Trials were arranged to take place in a public arena part way along the newly built L&MR on 14 October 1829. This contest sparked the interest of steam locomotive engineers and the public all over Britain.

The £5 note produced to commemorate George Stephenson. It shows *Locomotion* and *Rocket* as well as a passenger train passing over the Skerne river bridge on the S&DR. The Gaunless bridge is also depicted.

Rocket in the form in which it took part in the Rainhill Trials in October 1829. The sunflower-yellow livery was said to have been chosen because of the association with fast yellow stagecoaches of the time.

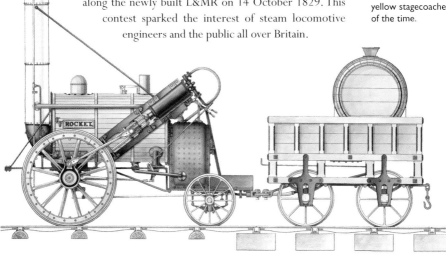

THE STEPHENSONS AND STEAM RAILWAYS BEFORE RAINHILL

Robert was different from his father, by education and the formative years of youth. Yet the two were one, inseparable in such a partnership as two strong characters have seldom achieved.

James A. Williamson

IN THE MINDS of many the name *Rocket* does not stand alone: to them it is the 'Stephensons' *Rocket*'. Many of them will be well aware that there were two great Stephensons, father and son, but fewer could confidently and correctly say which was responsible for *Rocket*. Writers and historians have over the years done more to confuse than clarify the situation. On the one hand, Samuel Smiles quoted Robert as saying: 'It was in conjunction with Mr Booth that my father constructed *Rocket*.' On the other hand, the authors of *Robert Stephenson, Railway Engineer* state: 'Contrary to popular belief George Stephenson had no involvement in the design and construction of Rocket...'

It is likely that what actually happened lies between these two extreme views. George and Robert regularly corresponded and visited each other while *Rocket* was being built in 1829 and, although there is no doubt that Robert constructed *Rocket* in Newcastle, he drew much from what George's hands had already built. The lives of the two Stephensons were intertwined with the development of steam locomotion and ultimately of *Rocket*, the machine that would change the world.

George was born in 1781 at Wylam, in coal-mining country 8 miles west of Newcastle-upon-Tyne. He was one of the six children of a poorly paid colliery engineman (another George) and learned about steam engines as a young lad, when he visited his father at work to take him his lunch. He grew up in humble surroundings, unable to read or write because his father could not afford to send him to school. As a youngster he got work labouring at the colliery where his father worked.

By the age of eighteen he had enrolled for night-school lessons from a local schoolmaster. All this time he was developing what would be a lifelong

Opposite:
Oil painting by William Lucas showing George Stephenson (1781–1848), seated, surrounded by his family and the symbols of his life's achievements – a colliery safety lamp and his first steam locomotive – on the wagonway at Killingworth Colliery near Newcastle.

George Stephenson and his son Robert were only twenty years apart in age and formed an unstoppable team in the early days of steam locomotion. Robert went on to outshine his father in later life as a very successful civil engineer.

George Stephenson's birthplace at Wylam is shown with a *Puffing Billy*-type locomotive standing outside. It is perhaps not surprising that, having a railway outside his door, George's interests developed the way they did.

passion for machinery and the new steam-driven technology. At the age of twenty-one he took charge of a local colliery's coal-loading equipment at Willington Quay.

At about this time George married Frances Henderson, and they lived close to his work. Their only child, Robert, was born in 1803, but tragically Frances died three years later of tuberculosis, leaving George as the sole carer and provider.

George's natural mechanical aptitude and ability gained him respect and early promotion at work. He worked hard to assimilate all the knowledge he could about mechanical devices and steam-driven equipment, and by the age of thirty he was distinguishing himself as an established engineer and mechanic. He started to consider the idea of using a steam locomotive to haul the laden coal wagons from the colliery down to the river.

George Stephenson, the 'Father of the Railways', depicted standing in front of his great civil-engineering achievement at Chat Moss.

George was not the inventor of the first steam locomotive. William Murdoch and Richard Trevithick had struggled with the concept and built rudimentary prototypes at the turn of the nineteenth century, and pioneers such as John Blenkinsop, William Hedley, William Chapman and John Buddle then developed machines for use in the collieries of Leeds and north-eastern England. But it was George Stephenson who effectively championed the concept of the steam locomotive and its railway as a complete unit.

11

Stephenson drew on the legacy of early pioneers of steam engines to replace horse power. One of the motivations for this was the high cost of animal feed for the railway operators following the Napoleonic Wars. Because of this, the steam locomotive's operating costs were competitive with horse-powered haulage. Steam locomotives could also work a lot longer than horses before getting exhausted.

Stephenson's first locomotive, *Blücher*, was built in 1814, and during the years from 1815 to 1825 he produced a series of locomotives to transport coal on the colliery railways of Killingworth and Hetton. All these locomotives were slow and clumsy and shared a basic design, having the cylinders and pistons located inside the boiler protruding outwards, and four wheels driven indirectly through a complex system of levers and links. The technology of smooth metal wheel on a smooth metal rail had only just been unlocked with an experiment carried out by William Hedley to show that iron wheels would indeed grip iron rails without slipping. It was thought to be remarkable that railway locomotive wheels did not lose grip when pulling a train.

It is believed that this watercolour painting was done by George Stephenson himself. It shows one of his Killingworth Colliery locomotives pulling loaded 'chauldron' wagons.

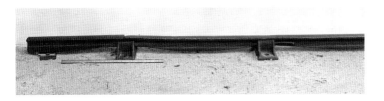

George Stephenson worked with William Losh to develop rails made from malleable iron to replace the brittle cast-iron sections that easily fractured. The new rails could take the weight of heavy steam locomotives.

Here we can see how the horse-worked railway differs fundamentally from the steam-worked one. The space between the tracks was for the horses to walk in, but when heavy locomotives came along the rails had to be supported by sleepers tying the track together.

Early engineers struggled with the challenge of their locomotives being too heavy for the track. Horses pulled wagons along by placing their own weight on the earth between tracks that were just strong enough to support a loaded wagon. But a locomotive capable of doing the work of the horse needed a heavy boiler and frame (weighing about three times as much as a loaded coal wagon, based on current crude stationary steam engine practice) carried on strong wheels.

The overloaded brittle cast-iron rails often broke under these locomotives. George Stephenson's solution was to work simultaneously on making 'malleable iron' rails with strong rail joints (manufactured from Swedish bar iron treated in a cementation furnace). These tracks carried the weight of his locomotives without fracturing.

Only twenty years younger than his father, Robert grew up very close to George and was always involved with his engines. However, George was

determined that his son would not suffer the deprivations of his own childhood and paid fees that he could ill afford to further Robert's continuing education at an academy in Newcastle. He used his mechanical ability to mend clocks and watches to supplement his wages. In Robert's early teens, his mathematical ability overtook his father's and they spent their evenings together sharing Robert's new knowledge.

When Robert was sixteen he started an apprenticeship at the Grand Allies Colliery. After completing this, he went to Edinburgh University to study mathematics and science. Meanwhile George was developing and improving his colliery locomotives and supplying his clients with a combined package of new railway infrastructure and locomotives. Previously, locomotives had been produced in colliery workshops using the readily available skills and techniques of the colliery's own blacksmith and millwright. When horses were used to pull wagons in a colliery, fodder had to be purchased, yet coal was in plentiful supply to fuel locomotives.

In 1825 a new railway was proposed to link the rich coalfields around Bishop Auckland with the river Tees at Stockton, called the S&DR. The Stephensons knew that colliery workshops would be inadequate and inappropriate for the building of the new locomotives as technologies became increasingly sophisticated, and in 1823 George, Robert and their partner Edward Pease set up a factory in Newcastle-upon-Tyne for manufacturing steam locomotives. They chose a site at Forth Street, and the new company was called Robert Stephenson & Company, demonstrating the strength of the partnership between father and son.

Robert had not been long in his new post as manager of the works before health problems started to affect his work. According to Samuel Smiles, 'to [Robert's] great relief, the doctor pronounced that a temporary residence in a warm climate was the very thing likely to be most beneficial to him'.

In April 1824 an opportunity arose for him to go, with his father's blessing, to South America to pursue mining interests – an early version of the 'gap-year' concept. Robert matured and flourished in a different and exciting environment. There is no doubt that he spent time thinking about how steam locomotives in England might be developed and improved. He became his own man while abroad, with his own strong views, and prepared to argue his corner, even with his father. For example, he wrote to him in 1828 of the need 'to reduce the size and ugliness of our travelling engines'.

The first locomotive for the newly created S&DR, *Locomotion*, was built in Newcastle in 1825, still in the style of George Stephenson's Hetton

The Robert Stephenson & Co works is still in existence in Newcastle-upon-Tyne and can be visited as part of a heritage trail. (The Robert Stephenson Trust.)

Colliery engines. But an important innovation in this machine was that the chain that previously coupled the two sets of driving wheels was replaced by horizontal connecting rods.

The familiar style of vertical cylinders mounted within the boiler was universal up to that time, but in *Locomotion* the wheels were mounted onto the boiler and the heavy chassis was dispensed with to save weight. The drive down to the wheels by long connecting rods driving onto cranks, like a vertical pedal car, was now well established and would prove to be one of the design faults of this early locomotive type.

Because of the harmful effect of the heavy early locomotives on the primitive track, there was an urgent need to reduce uneven loading. The early locomotives had rigid axle mountings with no springs and, just as a four-legged table on an uneven floor needs temporary packing to stop it pressing down on only three legs, so these locomotives needed axles that could move up and down but still carry their correct equal share of the weight. Stephenson experimented with steam springs and three-point suspension to ensure that all four wheels pressed on the track with constant minimal force. One problem was that the vertical driving rods caused variation in those forces on the wheels. Worse still, if the axles were put on springs, the increased vertical movement potentially allowed the pistons to smash into the ends of the cylinders. After a few abortive experiments to solve this problem, he made a breakthrough in 1827 with *LancashireWitch*, in which sloping cylinders appear for the first time.

George Stephenson's *Locomotion* was the locomotive used for the opening of the S&DR. The four-wheel drive was achieved by means of coupling rods rather than chains joining the wheels.

LIVERPOOL & MANCHESTER

RAIL WAY.

*The following is the Ordeal which we have decided each Locomotive Engine sha
undergo, in contending for the Premium of £500, at Rainhill.*

The weight of the Locomotive Engine, with its full compliment of water i
the boiler, shall be ascertained at the Weighing Machine, by eight o'clock i
the morning, and the load assigned to it, shall be three times the weight thereo
The water in the boiler shall be cold, and there shall be no fuel in the fire-plac
As much fuel shall be weighed, and as much water shall be measured an
delivered into the Tender Carriage, as the owner of the Engine may conside
sufficient for the supply of the Engine for a journey of thirty-five miles. Th
fire in the boiler shall then be lighted, and the quantity of fuel consumed fo
getting up the steam shall be determined, and the time noted.

The Tender Carriage, with the fuel and water, shall be considered to be, an
taken as part of the load assigned to the engine.

Those Engines that carry their own fuel and water, shall be allowed a pro
portionate deduction from their load, according to the weight of the engine.

The Engine, with the Carriages attached to it, shall be run by hand up to th
Starting Post, and as soon as the steam is got up to fifty pounds per square incl
the engine shall set out upon its journey.

The distance the Engine shall perform each trip, shall be one mile and thre
quarters each way, including one-eighth of a mile at each end for getting up th
speed, and for stopping the train, by this means the engine with its load, wi
travel one and a half mile each way at full speed

The Engine shall make ten trips, which will be equal to a journey of thirty
five miles, thirty mi es whereof shall be performed at full speed, and the averag
rate of travelling shall not be less than ten miles per hour.

As soon as the Engine has performed this task, (which will be equal to th
travelling from Liverpool to Manchester,) there shall be a fresh supply of fue
and water delivered to her, and as soon as she can be got ready to set out agair
she shall go up to the Starting Post, and make ten trips more, which will b
equal to the journey from Manchester back again to Liverpool.

The time of performing every trip shall be accurately noted, as well as th
time occupied in getting ready to set out on the second journey.

Should the Engine not be enabled to take along with it sufficient fuel an
water for the journey of ten trips, the time occupied in taking in a fresh suppl
of fuel and water, and shall be considered and taken as part of the time in per
forming the journey.

J. U. RASTRICK, Esq. Stourbridge, C. E.
NICHOLAS WOOD, Esq. Killingworth, C. E. } Judges.
JOHN KENNEDY, Esq. Manchester,

Liverpool, Oct. 6, 1829.

The sloping cylinder and cart-spring layout allowed the axles to follow undulations in the track without the driving forces jacking the locomotive up and down.

The furnaces on the early locomotives burned on a grate that was inside the single firetube that passed through the water-space of the boiler. *Lancashire Witch* was built with two separate firetubes within the boiler, side by side, each containing an independent fire. These tubes joined together outside the front of the boiler, to become the chimney. Had the significance of several separate tubes in boilers dawned on the designers? Perhaps they simply wished to avoid having to make a tricky hairpin bend in the firetube at the front of the boiler to return the flue to the chimney. Whatever the reason, it is significant that this arrangement allowed the driver and fireman to stand together at the same end of the machine. Maybe *Lancashire Witch* with its twin-flue boiler was the start of the thinking that later led Henry Booth (who was working very closely with both the Stephensons) to suggest the multi-tubular boiler as a way of improving the performance of the steam locomotive.

It was at this critical time that Robert returned from his three-year contract in South America to take his place at the head of the firm that bore his name. A letter from the Stephensons' partner, Edward Pease, to Robert urges:

> I can assure thee that the business at Newcastle as well as thy Father's engineering have suffered very much from thy absence and unless thou soon return the former will be given up. [Smiles, chapter XII.]

His return came only just in time. His father was fully involved with the problems of building the new L&MR, and Robert was able to give the locomotive-building business the close attention that it deserved. Father and son continued to keep up regular correspondence, as Robert forged ahead with locomotive development in Newcastle.

In 1829 the locomotive engineers of the day were challenged by the directors of the L&MR to produce their best locomotives to compete in public at what came to be known as the Rainhill Trials for a £500 prize. The Stephensons and their colleague Henry Booth decided to enter the competition. It was their big chance to show the world what steam locomotives were capable of.

Lancashire Witch is the missing link between *Locomotion* and *Rocket*. It even anticipated the multi-tubular boiler by having twin fires in tubes side by side.

Opposite:
The rules that the judges laid down for the competitors in the Trials stated that each locomotive must pull three times its own weight. On the day, the issue was confused by the weights of the tenders: *Novelty* did not have a tender, and concessions were made.

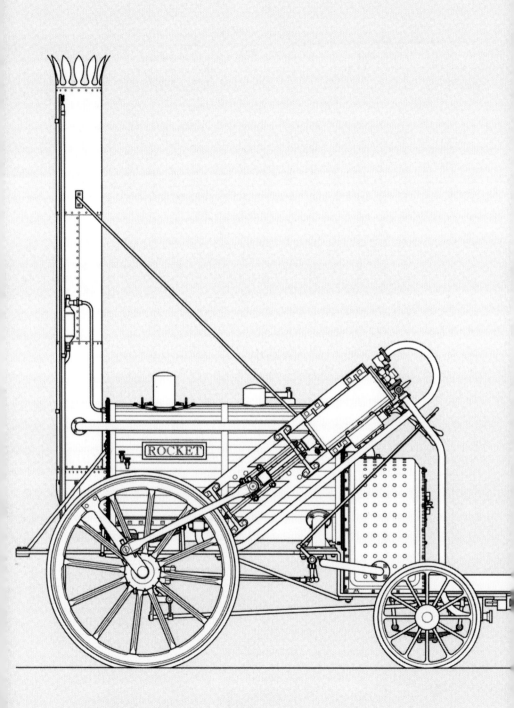

THE DESIGN OF ROCKET

THE RULES of the Rainhill Trials forced locomotive designers to come up with technical solutions which determined the form of the locomotives they submitted for trial. Mechanical reliability would be essential to cover 70 miles, which represented the distance from Liverpool to Manchester and back. More importantly, the steam production to drive the machine at the specified speed and power had to be sourced from the boiler continuously for several hours throughout the trial run.

The conditions limited the overall weight to $4^1/_2$ tons on four wheels. The wheels had to be carried on springs to lessen the possibility of track damage, and the boiler size had to be appropriate so that the locomotives would not overload the tracks. The Stephensons set out to create a high-powered lightweight machine, and it is remarkable, given that so little time was available to prepare for the Trials, that the design and layout of *Rocket* were so innovative. Because it was required to pull a train only three times its own weight, only the front pair of wheels needed to be powered. As they put the sloping cylinders near to the driver's controls, with short connecting pipes from the boiler, as in *Lancashire Witch*, a compact design emerged.

It was Henry Booth, the Secretary of the L&MR, who came up with what was probably *Rocket*'s single most important innovation. He advocated replacing the one large tube in which the fire burned on existing locomotives, with several smaller tubes to conduct the fire through the water boiling space. As Bailey and Glithero have shown, Booth used this idea to ally himself to George Stephenson and became a partner in the Trials venture. Once George Stephenson accepted that a high output boiler and external firebox were a practicable proposition, then Robert was also included in the partnership. Even though George was away in Liverpool building the railway, father and son kept in touch. George wrote to Robert about the design for *Rocket*: 'With respect to the engine for Liverpool I think the boiler ought not to be longer than eight feet. The engine ought to be made light as it is intended to run fast...'

Opposite:
Rocket drawn by John Glithero, showing the form of the machine as it competed in the Rainhill Trials in October 1829. The springs and the mercurial pressure gauge fastened to the chimney are visible.
(John P. Glithero.)

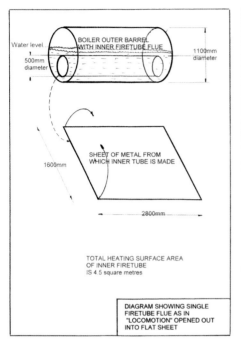

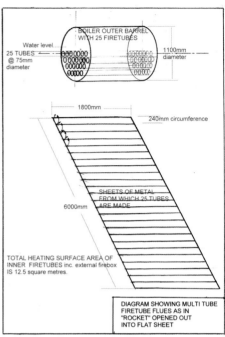

Above: Diagram by the author showing how the firetube for *Locomotion*'s boiler would have been made up from a flat sheet of metal. When complete, that tube would be surrounded by water on the outside and exposed to fire on the inside.

Above right: Diagram by the author showing how *Rocket*'s multi-tube boiler increased threefold the area of metal surfaces exposed to fire and water, even though the overall size of the boiler was much smaller than that of *Locomotion*.

It is hard to grasp the great leap forward that *Rocket* represented unless we understand the true significance of the multi-tube boiler on *Rocket*, compared with the single-flue boiler that went before, such as that used on *Locomotion*. The two boiler types are shown in the accompanying diagrams.

The heat from the fire in both examples is directly heating the inside surface of the tubes. The outside surface of the tubes is covered by water, as with the element in a kettle. The flames and hot gases from the fire will pass through the tubes and out at the other end up the chimney. Heat is conducted through the thickness of the metal tube wall to boil the water.

The diagrams show the size of the flat metal sheets needed to make the internal tubes on both types of boiler. *Locomotion*'s single tube, which has to end up at 500 mm in diameter, starts with a flat sheet approximately 1,600 mm wide and 2,800 mm long.

Now the tubes for the second boiler are only 75 mm in diameter, so for each tube a piece of metal 240 mm wide and the length of the boiler is required. But there are twenty-five of these tubes, so a piece of metal 6,000 mm wide and the length of the boiler is needed to make it. This is nearly three times the amount of metal exposed to the fire on one side and water on the other with the single flue, despite the multi-tube boiler being much smaller and lighter.

There are two additional bonuses. Firstly, overall weight is saved, because the multi-tube boiler holds 30 per cent less water than the single-flue version, as water is displaced by extra tubes; and the smaller tubes can be made of thinner metal, which means that heat can transfer across the metal thickness to the water more quickly. Weight-saving and steam production ability are two of the crucial points about the Stephensons' design.

Innovation was required at both ends in the new design of boiler. At the front, the twenty-five tubes containing waste gases had to be brought together to join the single chimney flue. A curved box was fashioned, to cover the ends of the flues and turn the hot gases into the tall chimney. At the rear, an external firebox was required to feed the heat to the ends of the tubes. This box was surrounded on three sides by a copper water jacket joined through circulating pipes to the main boiler barrel. The bottom of the box was formed by the grate, which supported the fire and allowed air to reach the burning fuel. Later on, as the designs became more sophisticated, this under-fire space was enclosed by an ash-pan to catch the burning cinders that fell through the firebars. The enclosed box also had a flap or 'damper' so that the fireman could control the rate at which the fire burned.

The multi-tube boiler was the design breakthrough that was needed to produce high power within the minimum overall weight, and *Rocket*, as shown at the start of this chapter, was what emerged from that process. We can speculate that without Booth's multi-tubular boiler contribution *Rocket* would have been built with a twin-flue boiler like that fitted to *Lancashire Witch*, and the outcome of the Rainhill Trials might have been very different.

Robert corresponded with his father, who was away in Liverpool for much of the time that *Rocket* was under development. He championed the idea of driving only one set of wheels to achieve a freer-running engine specifically for the Rainhill Trials, in which heavy load haulage was not the principal criterion for success. Many locomotives before and after Rainhill had all their carrying wheels coupled together for maximum haulage ability – the 1829 equivalent of a four-by-four vehicle.

The stipulated weight limit almost certainly influenced Robert to put *Rocket* on wooden driving wheels, with a wrought-iron hoop or tyre in contact with the rails. George had previously developed for *Locomotion* a standard cast-type of composite driving wheel made in two concentric rings held together by wooden plugs, but it was very heavy. Something lighter was needed for their racing machine at Rainhill.

The crude animal-derived lubrication available at the time limited the metal-to-metal sliding speeds, so the driving wheels needed to be large in order that the necessary intended high-vehicle speeds could be achieved with low-bearing speeds. Building large wooden road-vehicle wheels with

 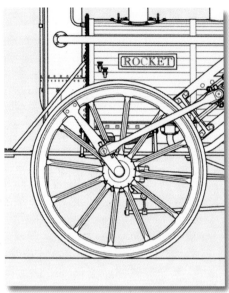

Above: Richard Trevithick's stationary steam engine of 1804 in the Science Museum. The engine's exhaust pipe was turned into the chimney on the right in order to get rid of the steam.

Above right: The driving wheel of *Rocket* as it was believed to have been at the time of the Rainhill Trials. The conventional wooden wheels would have been poor at carrying the pistons' reciprocating forces.

shrunk-on tyres was a well-developed technique, and this design was perfect for wheels drawn along by an external force. However, it was not a good method for transmitting turning forces from within the wheel such as Stephenson intended with his direct drive from the inclined cylinders. His solution was a metal strap connecting the wheel centre to the rim. The strap took the pushing and pulling forces from the pistons and placed the forces at the rim of the wheel, where they were needed, without straining the structure of the wheel.

Early locomotives exhausted their used steam from their cylinders straight into the atmosphere. It was the loud and explosive sounds of escaping steam that earned them a reputation for scaring people and animals. One solution was to deflect the exhaust from the cylinders into the chimney in order to act as a silencer.

The Stephensons went a stage further with the exhaust from *Rocket's* cylinders. The exhaust was admitted to the chimney through a vertically pointing nozzle at the end of each exhaust pipe. This had the effect of causing rapidly travelling 'billows' of exhausting steam to fill the chimney diameter and surge upwards to the top of the chimney, drawing the trapped hot flue gases behind it (akin to multiple corks being drawn in succession from a bottle). The vacuum pulses created in the base of the chimney drew fresh air in through the grate beneath the fire and caused the fire to burn more fiercely. The more the machine was driven towards its limit, the more power it produced.

THE DESIGN OF ROCKET

Great attention was paid, as we have seen, to making *Rocket* fast and reliable. Less thought was applied to making the locomotive stop. Given the tragedy that was later to unfold, it seems extraordinary to us nowadays that *Rocket* was built without brakes. It was possible to slow the train only by putting the engine into reverse and applying steam, a lengthy and tricky process. Carriages were equipped with parking brakes, but they were not under the control of the driver.

Design and manufacture complete, *Rocket* was put through satisfactory proving trials at Killingworth Colliery before being dismantled and sent to Liverpool ready to take part in the Rainhill Trials.

Rocket 's exhaust pipe set-up can be seen in the rectangular cutaway of the sectioned replica (more obvious in the illustration on page 48). Each exhaust pipe turns upwards inside the chimney and terminates in a nozzle to accelerate the steam.

A photograph of the erecting shop of Robert Stephenson's works in Newcastle-upon-Tyne taken in 1902 at the spot where the original *Rocket* was put together in 1829.

23

1829.

GRAND COMPETITION

OF

LOCOMOTIVES

ON THE

LIVERPOOL & MANCHESTER RAILWAY.

STIPULATIONS & CONDITIONS

ON WHICH THE DIRECTORS OF THE LIVERPOOL AND MANCHESTER RAILWAY OFFER A PREMIUM OF £500 FOR THE MOST IMPROVED LOCOMOTIVE ENGINE.

I.

The said Engine must "effectually consume its own smoke," according to the provisions of the Railway Act, 7th Geo. IV.

II.

The Engine, if it weighs Six Tons, must be capable of drawing after it, day by day, on a well-constructed Railway, on a level plane, a Train of Carriages of the gross weight of Twenty Tons, including the Tender and Water Tank, at the rate of Ten Miles per Hour, with a pressure of steam in the boiler not exceeding Fifty Pounds on the square inch.

III.

There must be Two Safety Valves, one of which must be completely out of the reach or control of the Engine-man, and neither of which must be fastened down while the Engine is working.

IV.

The Engine and Boiler must be supported on Springs, and rest on Six Wheels; and the height from the ground to the top of the Chimney must not exceed Fifteen Feet.

V.

The weight of the Machine, WITH ITS COMPLEMENT OF WATER in the Boiler, must, at most, not exceed Six Tons, and a Machine of less weight will be preferred if it draw AFTER it a PROPORTIONATE weight; and if the weight of the Engine, &c., do not exceed FIVE TONS, then the gross weight to be drawn need not exceed Fifteen Tons; and in that proportion for Machines of still smaller weight — provided that the Engine, &c., shall still be on six wheels, unless the weight (as above) be reduced to Four Tons and a Half, or under, in which case the Boiler, &c., may be placed on four wheels. And the Company shall be at liberty to put the Boiler, Fire Tube, Cylinders, &c., to the test of a pressure of water not exceeding 150 Pounds per square inch, without being answerable for any damage the Machine may receive in consequence.

VI.

There must be a Mercurial Gauge affixed to the Machine, with Index Rod, showing the Steam Pressure above 45 Pounds per square inch; and constructed to blow out a Pressure of 60 Pounds per inch.

VII.

The Engine to be delivered complete for trial, at the Liverpool end of the Railway, not later than the 1st of October next.

VIII.

The price of the Engine which may be accepted, not to exceed £550, delivered on the Railway; and any Engine not approved to be taken back by the Owner.

N.B.—The Railway Company will provide the ENGINE TENDER with a supply of Water and Fuel, for the experiment. The distance within the Rails is four feet eight inches and a half.

THE LOCOMOTIVE STEAM ENGINES,

WHICH COMPETED FOR THE PRIZE OF £500 OFFERED BY THE DIRECTORS OF THE LIVERPOOL AND MANCHESTER RAILWAY COMPANY.

DRAWN TO A SCALE ¼ INCH TO A FOOT.

THE "ROCKET" OF Mr. ROBt STEPHENSON OF NEWCASTLE,

WHICH DRAWING A LOAD EQUIVALENT TO THREE TIMES ITS WEIGHT TRAVELLED AT THE RATE OF 12½ MILES AN HOUR, AND WITH A CARRIAGE & PASSENGERS AT THE RATE OF 24 MILES. COST PER MILE FOR FUEL ABOUT THREE HALFPENCE.

THE "NOVELTY" OF MESSrs BRAITHWAITE & ERRICSSON OF LONDON,

WHICH DRAWING A LOAD EQUIVALENT TO THREE TIMES ITS WEIGHT TRAVELLED AT THE RATE OF 20¾ MILES AN HOUR, AND WITH A CARRIAGE & PASSENGERS AT THE RATE OF 32 MILES. COST PER MILE FOR FUEL ABOUT ONE HALFPENNY.

THE "SANSPAREIL" OF Mr. HACKWORTH OF DARLINGTON,

WHICH DRAWING A LOAD EQUIVALENT TO THREE TIMES ITS WEIGHT TRAVELLED AT THE RATE OF 12¾ MILES AN HOUR, COST FOR FUEL PER MILE ABOUT TWO PENCE.

THE RAINHILL TRIALS

WHY IN 1829 would the directors of the newly proposed L&MR, with their solid business sense, go to the trouble and expense of opening their trials of locomotives to the public? They could have managed the whole operation much more cheaply in private. Was it a publicity stunt to spread the word about the new railway, or was it a philanthropic gesture to share the new technology with an inquisitive public? We may speculate that Henry Booth, the Company Secretary, and George Stephenson persuaded each other that they had a world-beating idea and pushed for a way of demonstrating that in public.

The date chosen for the start of the trials was Tuesday 6 October 1829. A crowd of over ten thousand members of the public, as well as engineers and scientists, arrived at Rainhill, eager to witness this great event. A grandstand was built at the end of the marked course and the whole affair had the atmosphere of a large race meeting.

Three independent judges were appointed to oversee the trials. They were Nicholas Wood, John Raistrick and John Kennedy. We are fortunate that Raistrick made copious notes on the competitors and how they performed.

The judges chose as the trials course a level stretch of line 1¾ miles long at Rainhill, a few miles east of Liverpool. An accelerating and decelerating section one-eighth of a mile long was added to each end of the measured section, so that the competitors could change direction, yet still be timed at speed. Ten return trips equated to 35 miles, the distance between Liverpool and Manchester. Then, after a pause to take on fuel and water, the engines had to perform another ten return trips. Each locomotive had to pull a train of three times its own weight and keep up a minimum average speed of 10 mph over the timed section.

After demonstrations by the competitors on 6 October and rain on the 7th, the trials themselves spanned the 8 and 14 October 1829. Out of ten initial entries, only five made it to the actual competition, and only three were serious contenders: George and Robert Stephenson's *Rocket*,

Opposite:
This poster shows the three serious contenders in the Trials, and the text describes what the locomotives had to do to complete the trial. However, the casual stance of the well-dressed crews gives little indication that any them are about to undertake the 'Ordeal' that was in store.

Right: John Raistrick soon realised the significance of the multi-tube boiler. Here are his sketches and notes made during his inspections of *Novelty* at the Trials.

Below: John Raistrick, one of the judges, was very thorough in making extensive observations and sketches of how each locomotive worked. We are lucky that this notebook survives in the Science Museum's collections.

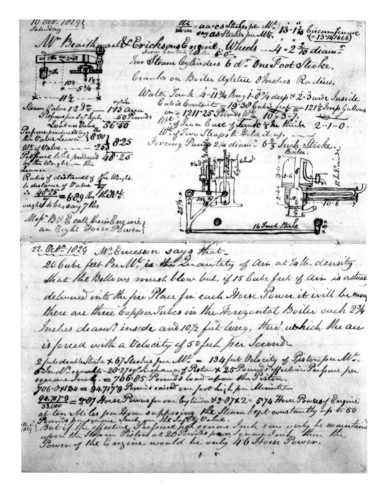

Timothy Hackworth's *Sans Pareil*, and John Braithwaite and John Ericsson's *Novelty*. Timothy Burstall entered his *Perseverance*, which was damaged during delivery, and Thomas Brandreth entered his two-horse-powered *Cycloped*, whose horses smashed through their treadmill early on. A sixth entrant, Ross Winans from the United States, with a two-man-powered locomotive, dropped out before the start.

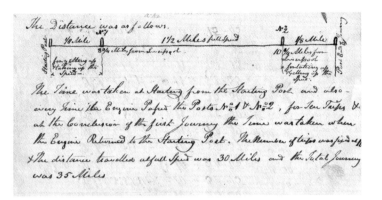

The rules stated that four-wheel locomotives had to carry their maximum weight of 4½ tons on springs to minimise track damage, and they had to burn coke rather than coal as fuel. This resulted from a rule stating that locomotives must 'consume their own smoke'. The railway company supplied standard wooden tenders that they had commissioned locally to act as water and coke carriers for the entrants. That is why the images of *Rocket* and *Sans Pareil* are seen with identical tenders attached. *Novelty*, *Perseverance* and *Cycloped* all carried their own provisions aboard the locomotive. An allowance for this measured weight difference was made by the judges in determining what loads each locomotive should have to draw.

On the first day *Rocket* and *Novelty* ran demonstrations for the crowd. On the second day *Rocket* competed in the proper trial and completed the two 35-mile measured sections, without mishap, in front of the appointed judges.

Drawing of *Rocket* done at the time of the Trials for the poster. It is fascinating that the driver and fireman in these views are depicted in such sartorial elegance – a far cry from the reality of the footplate.

Sans Pareil, with its vertical cylinders and no springs, showed its origins in an earlier generation of locomotives. The firetube arrangements banished the driver and fireman to opposite ends of the machine.

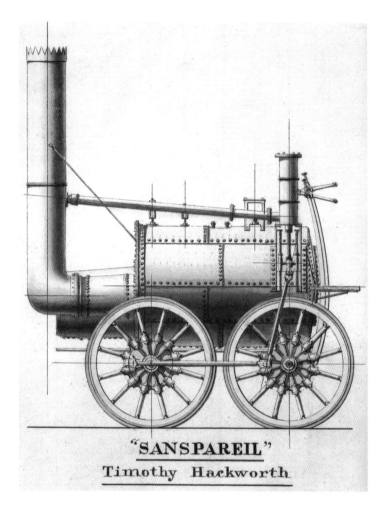

"SANS PAREIL"

Timothy Hackworth

The locomotive stopped for fourteen minutes between the two sections to take on coke and water. For the crowd watching from the stands, the speeds achieved, 24 mph maximum, with a 14 mph average, were spectacular.

On the third day it was *Novelty*'s turn to perform formally. The locomotive, with its absence of external moving parts and apparent simplicity, perhaps looked the most elegant of the three contenders. It seemed to win the crowd's affections as it attempted its trial. With the appropriate test load of nominally three times the weight of the locomotive, *Novelty* set off at a cracking pace. On the third leg of the trial, one of the crew inadvertently turned off the feed water to the boiler instead of diverting it back to the water tank. This caused the feed pipe to burst spectacularly

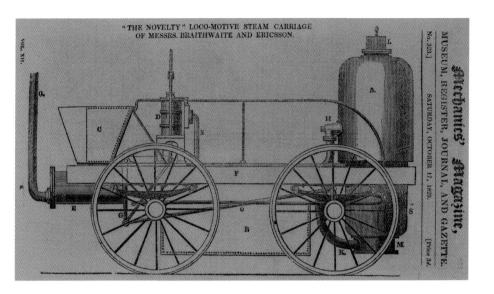

and the trial to be temporarily abandoned. It took nearly all day for the pipe to be mended. When the feed pipe was repaired, *Novelty* managed a demonstration run taking passengers at the astonishing rate of 30 mph. But all was not well: *Novelty*'s boiler had sustained damage through being temporarily starved of water when the pipe burst. Further repairs were necessary, which meant more delay. Meanwhile *Sans Pareil* was being frantically worked on by Hackworth to make it ready.

Although *Novelty* looks very simple and elegant, its boiler was very complex, and this view shows the chimney on the left at the far end of a long horizontal extension to the boiler. The bellows to blow the fire can be seen to the right of the chimney.

Timothy Burstall's *Perseverance* was dogged with bad luck. It overturned and sustained damage while being delivered to Rainhill. He spent most of the time trying to mend it. He did manage a 6 mph demonstration run.

Right: Cycloped was a treadmill powered by two horses. Although it did manage to operate, the amount of traction that the horses could impart to the moving belt was clearly limited. We know now that closer to ten horsepower was needed to do the job.

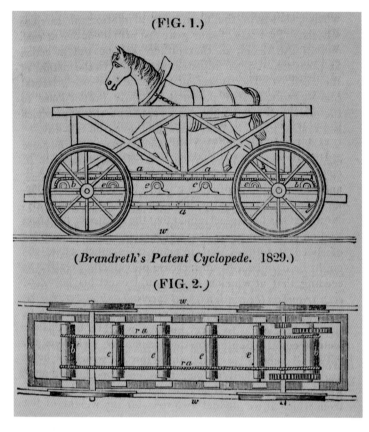

(FIG. 1.)

(*Brandreth's Patent Cyclopede.* 1829.)

(FIG. 2.)

Below: Timothy Hackworth was a disappointed competitor, but his achievement is remarkable nonetheless. He built *Sans Pareil* in his spare time while he was Chief Engineer of the S&DR. The Trials' outcome might have been different if his feed pump had not broken.

While the crowds were waiting, *Rocket* entertained them by giving rides and demonstrations. Passengers were carried up and down the nearby steep Whiston Incline on seats temporarily arranged in one of the test wagons. George Stephenson was able to demonstrate clearly to everyone present that his locomotive was capable of hauling trains up inclines that the directors had originally intended to operate with stationary engines.

At last Timothy Hackworth's *Sans Pareil* was ready to run. The repair of the engine in time for the Trials had presented Hackworth with a dilemma. He was scheduled to run on the second Monday, but as a devout Methodist he was unwilling to work on the Sunday. The judges were sympathetic enough to allow him a day's grace, to run on the following day.

Sans Pareil represented the final development of the 'old school' of colliery locomotive design and was technically ineligible because it was without springs and 600 pounds overweight – Hackworth claimed the scales were inaccurate. The judges nevertheless allowed it to run in the competition, and it performed well with good average speeds of up to 15 mph, but the locomotive was using excessive amounts of fuel.

Disaster struck just under half way through the course. The boiler feed pump smashed, starving the boiler of water. The top of the tube containing the fire lost its protective covering of water as the water level dropped, and Sans Pareil was forced to withdraw from the trial. Timothy Hackworth's dreams were over.

After further repairs Novelty started the Ordeal again. For the first few runs Braithwaite and Ericsson set a scorching pace, which pleased the crowd greatly. No doubt the Stephensons were agitated. But on the fourth leg of its first 35-mile journey an internal flue pipe collapsed in a huge cloud of steam, quenching the firebox and putting the people's favourite out of the running for good.

Viewed in retrospect, the outcome of the Trials was not always as clear as it might

Sans Pareil fortunately survived into preservation. It was reused as a water-pumping engine and lasted into an age when industrial artefacts were more valued. It is now one of the stars at Locomotion, the National Railway Museum's outstation at Shildon.

at first seem. *Novelty* was always the crowd's favourite to win, perhaps because its shape was reminiscent of an elegant horse-drawn carriage such as a landau. The other locomotives, with their tall chimneys, looked like nothing else they had ever seen. *Sans Pareil* put up a fair performance (in spite of a high fuel consumption), but technically things went catastrophically wrong for both *Novelty* and *Sans Pareil*. Braithwaite and Ericsson missed a real trick by not using the exhausting steam to draw the fire towards the chimney. *Novelty*'s pipework directed the spent steam downwards onto the track, doing no useful work, and the long horizontal flue gas passages from the fire wound a tortuous course through the boiler and would soon have choked up with ashes. A blast-pipe with its intermittent 'chuffing' would, no doubt, have kept these vital breathing passages clear. Although there was a bellows device assisting combustion of the fire, it did not match the 'throat-clearing' effect of the Stephensons' blast-pipe.

In contrast, *Rocket* put in a solid and reliable performance in the trial, which the Stephensons both knew would satisfy the judges, but they must have been deeply shocked when *Novelty* managed 30 mph in one of its warming-up runs. Indeed, George riskily uncoupled *Rocket* from its tender and test load during one of his demonstration runs and ran the locomotive at 35 mph to prove that his *Rocket* could not be outpaced.

The judges' report of 16 October 1829 stated:

> In conclusion we consider Mr Stephenson's Engine has completed in every respect with the Stipulations and Conditions issued by the Directors and dated 25th April 1829.

Below left:
John Braithwaite was a London-based engineer in partnership with John Ericsson, whose company built fire pumps. Their 'London Engine', *Novelty*, was put together in a matter of weeks.

Far right:
John Ericsson, Braithwaite's partner in the construction of *Novelty*, was a successful Swedish mechanical engineer who went on to become involved in naval warfare projects. The Monitor gun platform was one of his inventions.

The £500 prize was duly shared between George and Robert Stephenson and Henry Booth.

We are lucky to have a contemporary report of the Trials in an apparently reputable journal called the *Mechanics' Magazine*, which published twenty-six pages of detailed records of each day's activities. Its bias against the Stephensons' *Rocket* is fascinating. The report must have infuriated George and Robert when they read it:

> The directors had no alternative [to award the prize] since 'The Rocket' was the only engine that fulfilled the conditions of the competition. There are people here however who think that the interests of the public would have been quite as well served, had the directors adjudged the premium on a more general view of the matter, and conferred it on that engine which is on the whole 'the most improved'. [*Mechanics' Magazine*, Saturday 31 October 1829]

Clearly journalistic spin was alive and well in the early nineteenth century. Robertson, the editor of *Mechanics' Magazine*, who wrote this account, was a close friend of Braithwaite and obviously favoured the so-called 'London Engine', *Novelty*. Indeed, in later years he was to be discredited for shady dealings and bias. He certainly backed a loser when he wrote in the journal after the Trials had finished:

> '…and we believe we speak the opinion of nine-tenths of the engineers and scientific men now in Liverpool – that it is the principle and arrangement of this London engine which will be followed in the construction of all future locomotives.

Although the three principal locomotive contenders looked radically different in their appearance, they had similarly sized cylinders, wheels and drive mechanism, which determined their ability to get the train going. The inherent differences lay in their different boilers' ability to sustain a high output of steam production. Could this production keep pace with what the cylinders were using, and therefore keep the train running for 70 miles at speeds above 10 mph? It appears that only *Rocket* met that requirement completely, and it fully deserved the prize that was awarded.

ROCKET IN SERVICE AND AFTER

THE DIRECTORS of the L&MR purchased *Rocket*, the winner of the Trials, and placed orders for similar locomotives with Robert Stephenson's works. The new locomotives incorporated new ideas gained from the experience of operating *Rocket*, such as ash-pans to catch falling cinders, and smoke-boxes to collect particles in the flue gases, and *Rocket* itself was soon modified along the same lines.

Rocket's success generated a wave of interest in the new railway. Before it opened officially, rail tours behind Stephenson's locomotives from Liverpool to Rainhill and back were arranged for inquisitive people. The tours were part of a deliberate attempt to win the public relations battle for rail travel, but the public's reaction to the opportunity to travel so fast was mixed. The actress Fanny Kemble was wildly enthusiastic about her 35 mph footplate ride, with George Stephenson driving:

> I stood up, and with my bonnet off drank the air before me... When I closed my eyes this sensation of flying was quite delightful, and strange beyond description; yet strange as it was, I had a perfect sense of security, and not the slightest fear... Now a word or two about the master of all these marvels with whom I am most horribly in love... He is a man from fifty to fifty five years of age; his face is fine, though careworn, and very original, striking and forcible... He has certainly turned my head.

Thomas Creevey MP, a vocal railway opponent, was rather less enthusiastic. He reported on his train ride (at 23 mph):

> But the quickest motion is to me frightful; it really is flying, and it is impossible to divest yourself of the notion of instant death to all upon the least accident happening. It gave me a headache which has not left me yet.

When the new and more powerful locomotives were delivered to the railway from Robert Stephenson's works, they were better suited to pulling

Opposite:
As present-day passengers travel along Olive Mount Cutting into Liverpool, the chisel marks where these workmen hacked out the stone can still be seen and admired. Surely the working practices depicted here would have been recognised as dangerous even in 1829. We can only speculate what *Rocket*'s fireman is saying to his top-hatted colleague!

Rocket at the Moorish Arch in Liverpool with a passenger train. The condition of the locomotive as depicted, would suggest that this is the sight that would have greeted Fanny Kemble or Thomas Creevey on their rides with *Rocket* with George Stephenson. (Rainhill Railway and Heritage Society.)

heavy trains and, even before the opening of the line, *Rocket* was relegated to lighter duties, such as delivering materials for George Stephenson's civil engineering challenge to complete a floating railway line across Chat Moss, a notorious bog near Irlam. Stephenson's infrastructure still carries today's L&MR.

The official opening of the railway took place on 15 September 1830. It was a very grand affair, attended by many important people. The principal guest was the Prime Minister, the Duke of Wellington, in whose train, pulled by *Northumbrian*, there were over seven hundred guests. The Duke's carriage was an ostentatious construction with gilt mouldings and a canopy. To maximise the visual spectacle, George Stephenson had arranged for the eight special trains scheduled to make the opening run to travel in the same direction on the two tracks from Liverpool to Manchester and back.

Fanny Kemble was an actress appearing in a Liverpool production at the time between the Trials and the railway's opening, when trains were being demonstrated. Fanny was bowled over by her ride on *Rocket's* footplate with George Stephenson. (Topfoto/The Granger Collection.)

When the cavalcade stopped at Parkside, 17 miles from Liverpool, for the locomotives to take water to complete the journey, there was a brief opportunity for guests to

Chat Moss, impassable bogland in the path of the proposed railway near Irlam. Stephenson created a brushwood embankment, which still supports the present Liverpool to Manchester line.

A painting that purports to show *Rocket* at the time of the public running exercise to win hearts and minds before the Grand Opening. Examination shows that this is in fact *Northumbrian*, one of the new Robert Stephenson locomotives delivered in 1830.

The Grand Opening procession of eight trains about to set off from Liverpool for Manchester. The extra-wide Prime Minister's carriage, which caused William Huskisson MP to become trapped at Parkside, can be seen.

dismount from the trains and circulate. William Huskisson, MP for Liverpool, was anxious to greet the Prime Minister and be seen with him. As he was conversing with the Duke beside the track, he was trapped in the gap formed between the extra-wide carriage and the approaching *Rocket* pulling in to Parkside. Huskisson panicked and fell back across the track. One of his legs was crushed by *Rocket*'s driving wheel.

The celebratory mood changed rapidly as the extent of Huskisson's injuries and the need to get medical help for him was realised. *Northumbrian* was uncoupled from the Duke's train and, with George Stephenson driving, rushed the injured man to Manchester. It was no consolation that Stephenson's mercy dash driving *Northumbrian* ran at nearly 40 mph, faster than any human being had previously travelled. Tragically, later that day, William Huskisson died and became the world's first recorded railway accident fatality. Although the retinue continued to Manchester as planned, the festivities were curtailed. The Grand Opening had been marred and subdued guests returned to Liverpool.

Huskisson's tragic death started a seventy-five-year long quest to improve the ability of trains to stop in an emergency, but it would take another thirteen years of development before locomotives could be 'thrown into

ORDERS OF THE DAY.

LIVERPOOL, SEPTEMBER 13th, 1830.

The Directors will meet at the Station, in Crown Street, not later than Nine o'clock in the Morning, and during the assembling of the Company will severally take charge of separate Trains of Carriages to be drawn by the different Engines as follow :—

NORTHUMBRIAN	*Lilac Flag.*	Mr. Moss.
PHŒNIX	*Green Flag.*	Mr. Earle.
NORTH STAR	*Yellow Flag.*	Mr. Harrison.
ROCKET	*Light Blue Flag.*	Mr. A. Hodgson.
DART	*Purple Flag.*	Mr. Sandars.
COMET	*Deep Red Flag.*	Mr. Bourne.
ARROW	*Pink Flag.*	Mr. Currie.
METEOR	*Brown Flag.*	Mr. David Hodgson.

The men who have the management of the Carriage-breaks will be distinguished by a white ribbon round the arm.

When the Trains of Carriages are attached to their respective Engines a Gun will be fired as a preliminary signal, when the "Northumbrian" will take her place at the head of the Procession ; a second Gun will then be fired, and the whole will move forward.

The Engines will stop at Parkside (a little beyond Newton) to take in a supply of water, during which the company are requested not to leave their Carriages.

At Manchester the Company will alight and remain one hour to partake of the Refreshments which will be provided in the Warehouses at that station. In the farthest warehouse on the right hand side will be the Ladies' Cloak Room.

Before leaving the Refreshment Rooms a Blue Flag will be exhibited as a signal for the Ladies to resume their Cloaks ; after which the Company will repair to their respective Carriages, which will be ranged in the same order as before ; and sufficient time will be allowed for every one to take his seat, according to the number of his Ticket, in the Train to which he belongs ; and Ladies and Gentlemen are particularly requested not to part with their Tickets during the day, as it is by the number and colour of the Tickets that they will be enabled at all times to find with facility their respective places in the Procession.

Left: The orders for the Grand Opening procession. The eight locomotives with their flag colours are specified. It is a shame that William Huskisson ignored the plea for 'the company not to leave their carriages' when the trains stopped at Parkside to take water.

Below: A ticket for the opening cavalcade. The document specifies the seat number, the flag colour of the particular train and the name of the locomotive pulling that train. It was clearly a well-organised affair.

Opening

OF

THE LIVERPOOL AND MANCHESTER RAILWAY,

WEDNESDAY, 15TH SEPTEMBER, 1830.

CHAS. LAWRENCE, CHAIRMAN.

THE BEARER OF THIS TICKET IS ENTITLED TO SEAT No.

NORTH STAR'S TRAIN.

YELLOW FLAG.

ENT?

PARKSIDE STATION

Left: Parkside station, where it all went so badly wrong on the opening day. Huskisson was trapped between the Prime Minister's extra-wide carriage and *Rocket* with its train passing on the other track.

William Huskisson MP, who was so keen to use the opportunity of the Grand Opening to patch up his relationship with the Prime Minister. He became the first recorded passenger fatality on a railway, run down by *Rocket*.

A scene at Parkside station with a *Planet*-type Stephenson locomotive at the head of the train, and showing the water column where engines filled up their tenders. Note the guard-operated brake on the coach wheel.

reverse', with the locomotive wheels madly slipping backwards, to stop the train. At Stephenson's insistence, handbrakes started to appear on locomotives delivered after 1831.

After the opening, *Rocket* continued to be used on the railway but became increasingly less useful as train weights increased. Robert Stephenson ran a successful development programme for his new locomotive designs, culminating in *Planet* of 1830. Even though only a couple of years separate them, *Planet* represents a huge technological leap forward from *Rocket*. The unique and strange-looking *Rocket* profile was left behind as the now familiar steam locomotive outline emerged for the first time. *Planet*, like *Rocket*, was supplied without brakes, although an image of *Planet* and train at Parkside station shows no tender brake but a handbrake on the carriages of the train.

By 1834 there was little work for *Rocket*, and it was offered as a test bed for a novel sort of drive system, which was found to be unsuccessful. Afterwards the locomotive went back to being stored out of use.

In 1836 *Rocket* was restored for sale, and a drawing was made at this time. This clearly illustrates the changes that had been made to the engine as it

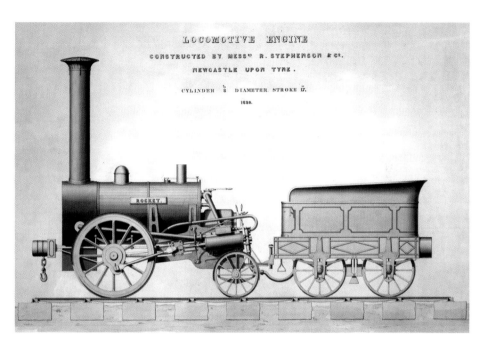

was repaired on several occasions following a number of minor accidents and incidents over its seven years of Liverpool & Manchester service.

Rocket was sold to the Earl of Carlisle's colliery in Cumberland, where it continued to work pulling coal trains until sold again in 1838 to J. Thompson, another colliery owner. By 1840 it had been withdrawn from active service, and in 1851 it was returned to the Robert Stephenson factory in the hope that it could be exhibited at the Great Exhibition, but somehow this never happened. In 1862, however, it was transferred to the Patent Office Museum's collection, which was to become the Science Museum in 1909. Attempts by the museum to make the remains of *Rocket* more representative of the original machine raised the great curatorial dilemma that affects any object that has been greatly modified during its working life. *Rocket* had acquired its iconic status at Rainhill in 1829, yet by 1862 it was barely recognisable. What stage of its continually changing life should the locomotive represent when displayed in the museum? To have rebuilt it at that stage back in its 1829 form would have involved major surgery, the removal of some genuine post-1829 components and their replacement with facsimiles. The solution adopted at the time was to replace some of the missing components such as the connecting rods and firebox with wooden replicas. By 1935 these alterations were recognised as misleading and were removed.

The 1836 drawing of *Rocket* when it was ready to be sold to the Earl of Carlisle. After only seven years of use, *Rocket* is barely recognisable with its new smokebox, chimney, lowered cylinder position and front buffer-beam.

The 1840 Robert Stephenson & Co drawing of *Rocket*, showing the condition of the locomotive at the time of its withdrawal from service. That such a drawing was done suggests that the locomotive had special status even then.

Rocket is now one of the star attractions in a gallery called 'Making the Modern World' at the Science Museum in London, but its subdued appearance gives few hints of the storm of excitement it caused when it first appeared brightly coloured at Rainhill in 1829 in front of the crowds of spectators.

This view of *Rocket* as it was first displayed at the Patent Office Museum in 1876 shows the unsuccessful attempts to make what remained of the locomotive resemble more closely its appearance at the Rainhill Trials.

The Stephensons' *Rocket* as displayed in 'Making the Modern World' at the Science Museum in 2006. So much is missing or has been replaced that it is challenging to recreate the excitement of this machine racing at Rainhill in 1829.

In 1999 a significant project, in effect an archaeological investigation, to understand *Rocket* better was carried out by Dr Michael Bailey and John Glithero at the National Railway Museum in York. Much of value about the engineering history of *Rocket* was discovered and published. For example, it was during this research that it was discovered that the locomotive suffered three accidents in its early working life. The frame was bent, and fractured whilst being straightened, and one of the driving wheels was replaced. The original copper firebox was found to have been manufactured crooked, as a consequence of which the locomotive frame had to be modified to accept it.

John Glithero and Dr Michael Bailey carrying out their archaeological investigation of *Rocket*'s remains at the National Railway Museum in 1999. This was carried out in the public area and findings were shared with the public daily.

THE LEGACY OF THE STEPHENSONS' ROCKET

A S WE HAVE SEEN, *Rocket* lasted only a short time in the service of the L&MR, and even in industrial service its working life was brief. But the engine lived on, in more ways than one.

The Rainhill Trials made *Rocket* famous, but the fame of the engine increased as the years passed. Early historians of the railways gave *Rocket* a special place at the roots of the locomotive family tree. Every locomotive that the Victorians produced was *Rocket*'s descendant, and the successor companies of the Liverpool & Manchester soon realised that to claim ownership of *Rocket* and its direct 'blood line' was a powerful marketing tool. As early as 1881, the Crewe works of the London & North Western Railway (LNWR) built what would be the first of several full-size replicas of *Rocket*. This and the image of *Rocket* were used by the company to assert its claim to be the 'Premier Line' and among the greatest innovators of the modern world. The LNWR's successor, the London Midland & Scottish Railway (LMS), followed suit, using *Rocket* to indicate that the LMS was not only the most modern of the 'Big Four' railway companies but had the most authentic pedigree.

When the American motor industry magnate Henry Ford commissioned Robert Stephenson & Co to make him an exact replica of *Rocket* for his museum of engineering in Detroit in 1929, he wanted to place it in a hall of fame showing the landmarks of the Industrial Revolution, of which his Ford Motor Company represented the newest chapter. Like the LNWR, Henry stood to profit by associating himself with the Stephensons' landmark, but *Rocket*, too, became more famous as a result. The legend grew and grew.

Henry Ford was fascinated by the development of production techniques, and his replica was built with the greatest care, using techniques that fell out of favour soon after the original *Rocket* was made. The resulting engine provides a unique technological record for future generations. Take, for example, the twenty-five copper tubes of the multi-tubular boiler. In Ford's replica each tube was painstakingly rolled up out of flat copper sheets and brazed together by hand to form 3-inch diameter tubes, though it would have been easy to buy ready-made 3-inch diameter seamless copper pipe in 1929. All screws

Opposite:
The 2010 brochure for the National Railway Museum in York depicts today's children drawn to *Rocket* in the form of the sectioned replica. The Stephensons' iconic machine is still drawing crowds after 181 years.

45

This photograph is claimed to show George Stephenson himself with the original *Rocket* from the very early days of photography. We know it is a fake because the shape of the firebox should not slope as shown.

used on the replica were laboriously cut by hand. We must be grateful for Henry Ford's exacting standards, for our interaction with the replica locomotives offers rare insights into the manufacturing processes of the period in which the original *Rocket* was built.

Ford's *Rocket* was certainly the finest version of the engine then seen in the United States, but it was not the first. In 1923 a replica was made to appear in Buster Keaton's film *Our Hospitality*. It is testament to the fame of the engine that a Hollywood studio should have chosen *Rocket* as its star, in a film based in the Wild West, far distant from Rainhill. Once again, the legend of *Rocket* was reinforced.

Keaton's *Rocket* was an approximation in wood that achieved feats of comedic running that could not be matched by the real thing, but it was Henry Ford's replica that would have the greater significance: three further replicas were commissioned from Robert Stephenson & Co during the 1930s, all of them built with the same care and attention to detail that had been lavished on the Detroit engine. One complete locomotive went to the Chicago Museum of Science and Industry, and sectioned examples were made for the Museum of the Peaceful Arts in New York (later the New York Museum of Science and Industry) and the Science Museum in London.

Two of these engines were made to be fully operational but they were destined for museum display. It would not be until the 1970s that a replica of

Above: This photograph taken in Blackpool in 1923 shows a pageant float about to set off with a replica *Rocket* on the back of the horse-drawn wagon.

Rocket was constructed that would run regularly and would, 150 years after its ancestor took to the rails, teach us much about *Rocket* that had long been forgotten.

Replicas can fulfil far more exciting roles if they can be operated. They offer insights into how technology changed the lives of communities. The Norwegian explorer Thor Heyerdahl found this when his full-sized balsa-wood raft was used to prove that in pre-Columbian times people from

Robert Stephenson & Co went on to build huge numbers of full-sized locomotives to be exported all over the world. This one is shown new alongside one of the replica *Rockets* produced at the same time. (Graeme Pilkington.)

South America could have settled in Polynesia using existing technology. In the case of *Rocket*, we have learned things from the operation of the National Railway Museum's replica that help shed light on the story recounted in this book. For example, those familiar with driving replicas of *Rocket* can appreciate the way that *Rocket*'s inadequate reversing mechanism contributed to the tragic death of William Huskisson on the opening day of the L&MR. We can be certain that the driver, Joseph Locke, jumped quickly on the reversing pedal to change *Rocket*'s valve gear from forward to reverse when he saw Huskisson in front of his locomotive, but we know that the deceleration of the engine would have been far from instantaneous. Locke did not experience in time that feeling of relief familiar to drivers who have tried to halt replicas of *Rocket* as the gear drops into place to pull the locomotive to a controlled halt.

In 1980 a pageant was staged at Rainhill to celebrate the passage of 150 years since the opening of the L&MR. Working replicas of all three serious contenders were built, including *Rocket*. On this occasion the engines did not compete, but in 1999 the BBC proposed a re-staging of the trials for the *Timewatch* programme. The re-run would use the replica

The 1935 replica *Rocket*, which was supplied sectioned by Robert Stephenson & Co so that observers could see inside the multi-tube boiler and cylinders to understand more fully how the locomotive works.

locomotives to see if the outcome would be the same as in 1829, and three tough and knowledgeable judges would enforce the original Rainhill Trials rules. There were many observers present who wanted to see the course of history changed in the re-enactment, but *Rocket* did win the competition again, although, as in 1829, the teams faced some tough technical challenges to get their locomotives to the end of the course.

In the second decade of the twenty-first century we have the opportunity to learn even more about *Rocket*, as the working replica is rebuilt with an exact copy of its original boiler, and various other modifications inspired by the archaeology that was carried out on the original engine. Time will tell what we may yet have to learn.

The Science Museum's sectioned replica being erected at the works of Robert Stephenson & Co in 1935 to Henry Ford's exacting specification. This photograph came to light during research for this book. (*The Northern Echo* and Don Whitfield.)

FOR OVER
ONE HUNDRED YEARS
IN PEACE AND WAR

L M S

The 1930 Crewe Rocket replica with the London Midland & Scottish Railway's latest product to celebrate their centenary.

49

The Museum of British transport, Clapham, London had a replica Rocket displayed on stilts until it closed in 1973. This replica was used to make the working replica of 1979 at Springwell workshops in County Durham.

Nothing can take away *Rocket*'s place as one of the most important of all railway vehicles, and truly one of the makers of the modern world. Its true significance might not quite match up to the legend that has been built around it, but it is indisputable that the three great developments embodied in *Rocket* for the first time – the blast-pipe, the multi-tube boiler and the sloping cylinders with direct drive – became the basis of best practice in steam locomotive design for 130 years, and made possible the successful development of railways and everything that the railway revolution brought. No railway locomotive has left a more enduring legacy to the world.

If George and Robert Stephenson could have been magically transported through time to 1960 and onto the footplate of the very last steam locomotive produced for British Railways, *Evening Star*, there is no doubt that they would have recognised it as derived from their original locomotive, *Rocket*. I like to believe that the combination of father and son would have been able to drive *Evening Star* away. They would certainly have been stopped in their tracks to see the remains of their original Rainhill racing locomotive *Rocket* attracting large crowds as one of the key exhibits at the Science Museum in South Kensington. Did they ever know that they had built such a legend?

Above: The National Railway Museum's *Rocket* replica in steam at the museum coupled to one of two replica L&MR coaches built for the Liverpool and Manchester Railway centenary in 1930, named *Traveller* and *Huskisson*.

Below: The *Rocket* replica at the 1980 'Rocket 150' celebrations. The event, with grandstands to accommodate the visitors, was also held at Rainhill.

Left: The National Railway Museum's *Rocket* replica ready to take part in the re-run of the Rainhill Trials staged by the BBC in 2002. (All images on this page courtesy of Martyn Stevens.)

Below left: The Timothy Hackworth Museum's replica *Sans Pareil* and crew ready for action. The driver and fireman were at opposite ends of the locomotive.

Below right: The Swedish National Railway Museum's replica *Novelty*, ready to take part in the trials. The crew was authentically half-Swedish, to maintain tradition.

Above: The three contenders line up at the start of the re-run of the Rainhill Trials for the BBC. The event was filmed at the Llangollen Railway, where similar conditions to the Rainhill level section were identified.

Above right: Here is evidence of the multi-tubular boiler's capability. During the re-run trials, *Rocket* worked so hard that the flames came right through the twenty-five tubes and set fire to the debris in the chimney.

Above: The external firebox was rebuilt with an authentic copper version shaped as the original. The water circulation pipes joining it to the multi-tubular boiler can be seen bottom left and top centre. (Both images on this page courtesy of the author.)

Above: *Rocket* Still entertaining the crowds in 2010. The National Railway Museum's recently rebuilt replica with its new more accurate boiler fitted, gives rides to the standing public (4th class!) at the Museum. The passengers get a good view of how the Stephensons drove their own locomotive at the Rainhill Trials. (Lesley Doubleday)

Left: In 2010 the National Railway Museum's replica *Rocket* was rebuilt at Bill Parker's Flour Mill in the Forest of Dean. New Frames and trailing wheels together with a new boiler which closely followed Stephenson's original design brought the replica much closer to its ancestor.

FURTHER READING

Bailey, Michael, and Glithero, John. *The Engineering and History of 'Rocket':
A Survey Report.* Science Museum, 2000.
Bailey, Michael, and Glithero, John. *The Stephensons' 'Rocket':A History of a
Pioneering Locomotive.* Science Museum, 2002.
Charlton, L. G. *The First Locomotive Engineers.* Graham, 1974.
Garfield, Simon. *The Last Journey of William Huskisson.* Faber & Faber, 2002.
McGowan, Christopher. *The Rainhill Trials:The Birth of Commercial Rail.*
Little, Brown, 2004.
Skeat, W. O. *George Stephenson:The Engineer and His Letters.* Mechanical
Engineering Publications, 1973.
Smiles, Samuel. *Lives of the Engineers: George and Robert Stephenson.* London,
1874.
Smiles, Samuel. *The Life of George Stephenson.* London, 1857.
Thomas, R. H. G. *The Liverpool and Manchester Railway.* Batsford, 1980.
Westcott, G. F. *The British Railway Locomotive 1803–1853.* Her Majesty's
Stationary Office, 1958.
Williamson, James A. *George and Robert Stephenson.* Black, 1958.

PLACES TO VISIT

Baltimore & Ohio Railway Museum, 901 West Pratt Street, Baltimore,
Maryland 21223, USA.
Forth Street Works, Newcastle-upon-Tyne.
Locomotion – National Railway Museum, Hackworth Close, Shildon, County
Durham DL4 1PL. Telephone: 01388 777999.
Website: www.locomotion.uk.com
Middleton Top Engine House, Cromford, Derbyshire.
The Museum of Science and Industry in Manchester, Liverpool Road,
Castlefield, Manchester M3 4EP. Telephone: 061883 0027.
Website: www.mosi.org.uk
National Railway Museum, Leeman Road, York YO26 4XJ.
Telephone: 08448 153139. Website: www.nrm.org.uk
Rainhill Railway Museum, View Road, Rainhill, Prescot, Merseyside L35 0LE.
The Science Museum, Exhibition Road, South Kensington, London SW7 2DD.
Telephone: 0870 870 4868. Website: www.sciencemuseum.org.uk
Sheep Pasture incline, Cromford, Derbyshire.
Swedish National Railway Museum, Gävle, Sweden.

LIST OF FULL-SIZE REPLICAS OF ROCKET

Date – Manufacturer – Type – For whom made – Present location - Comments

1881 – Crewe Locomotive Works – Non-working – London & North Western Railway – n/a – Wood and metal replica built by Francis Webb for Stephenson Centenary in 1881 and later exhibited by the LNWR at the Columbian World's Exposition, Chicago, 1893. Rebuilt in the same form in 1911. Modified more closely to resemble Rocket as-built *c.* 1930, and exhibited at Liverpool and Manchester Railway centenary celebrations in Liverpool. Exhibited at Museum of British Transport, Clapham, 1963–73. Scrapped in 1970s, donating some parts to 1979 working replica.

1892 – Mount Clare Workshops, Maryland – Wooden – Columbian World's Exposition/Baltimore and Ohio Railroad – Current location/status unknown – Initiative of Colonel J. G. Pangborn. Built for World's Columbian Exposition in Chicago, 1893, and exhibited again at 1927 Baltimore and Ohio Railroad 'Fair of the Iron Horse'.

1923 – Buster Keaton and Joseph M. Schenk Productions, Hollywood – Non-steam, operable – Film prop for 'Our Hospitality' – Current location/status unknown – Also used as a prop in 'The Iron Mule'.

1929 – Robert Stephenson & Co, Darlington; order E137; works no. 3992 – Operable – Henry Ford – Henry Ford Museum, Dearborn, Michigan – On display.

1930 – T. Robinson, Liverpool – Non-working – London Midland & Scottish Railway – n/a – Wooden prop made for the 'Pageant of Transport' at Liverpool and Manchester Railway centenary celebrations, Liverpool. Probably scrapped, 1930s.

1930 – Robert Stephenson & Co, Darlington; order E149; works no. 4071 – Sectioned – Museum of the Peaceful Arts, New York – Current location unknown – Exhibited at Museum of Science and Industry at the Rockefeller Center, New York, then sold to Bill Harrah in 1950. Later part of Jasper Wiglesworth collection and sold at auction in 2004 to unknown buyer.

1931 – Robert Stephenson & Co, Darlington; order E150; works no. 4072 – Operable – Museum of Science and Industry, Chicago – Museum of Science and Industry, Chicago – On display.

1935 – Robert Stephenson & Co, Darlington; order E155; works no. 4089 –Sectioned – Science Museum, London – National Railway, Museum, York – On display.

1979 – Locomotion Enterprises, Springwell Workshops, Bowes Railway, County Durham – Operable – Science Museum and National Railway Museum – n/a – Built by Michael Satow using wrought iron frames, springs and carrying wheelsets from 1881 replica for 'Rocket 150' celebrations in 1980. Operated all over the world. Dismantled in 2009.

2010 – The Flour Mill, Bream, Gloucestershire – Operable – Science Museum and National Railway Museum – National Railway Museum, York – Built by Bill Parker using driving wheels, cylinders and other components from 1979 replica.

INDEX